CW01497521

NOTES *of* YOUR MUSIC

Notes of Your Music

JAMES NASH

VP

First published in 2025 by Valley Press
Woodend, The Crescent, Scarborough, UK, YO11 2PW
valleypressuk.com

ISBN 978-1-915606-45-7
Cat. no. VP0237

Cover and text design by Jamie McGarry.
Cover illustration by Jacky Fleming.

Printed and bound in Great Britain by
TJ Books, Padstow, Cornwall.

Contents

Introduction

Is this the most challenging collection that I have written and put together so far? I suspect I think that every time I get involved in this process – when I experience the dry periods, the impostor syndrome that always perches on my shoulder, the emotional journey of it all, and the fluctuations in inspiration which make me question whether the latest poem written was indeed the final one that I will ever write.

Sometimes being asked to write a poem, as a commission or for a friend, can provide its own impetus and I am placed in that tentative, creative stage which can feel slightly dangerous, often delightful and full of promise.

The poems in this collection are bookended by older ones; a line from 'Petals' provided the title for this collection (and part of the inscription on the back of 'my seat' in the new screening room of my beloved Hyde Park Picture House) and 'Autumn' a last whisper of mortality, if you like, the preoccupying theme of many creative artists.

Thanks go to my best of editors Jo Brandon, to Jacky Fleming for her sublime cover illustration (the tune is 'Top Hat' by Irving Berlin if you're asking), to Jason Edwards who has supported me throughout my writing career, to Jack Haworth for the bike rides and the brilliant chats, and to 'the blackbird lighting up with sudden song' who is my fabulous husband David Robinson, supportive and creative in every way.

James Nash, 2025

Petals – a preface

Remember the music we used to play?
The instruments still hang on the wall,
a trellis of brass roses
or an exotic vine with bugle flowers.
Like plumbing but not joined up,
and silent now.
And the lid of the piano is down.

The tunes still prickle in my blood,
and though blooming less
each successive year,
have kept a scent of you.
And the truth is
that I have grown older and loved others,
but I shall always carry some notes of your music
in my pockets, like petals,
wherever I go.

This Resolution

This resolution to write more, to chase
Away the shadows, comes with fear.
I hope for a kindly, creative space
Where I can heal myself, where I can dare
To think and write again, to cast off
The fractures of the past, or celebrate
Their complex patterns, the tightly woven stuff
Of a lived life, that can chafe and fret.
For it comes with dangers, the possibility
Of a dark alley mugging, the bruised skin
And the traps of a past life that I can't foresee
That might not free but chain my nightmares in.
But I will try to keep this promise that I give
And explore the life I've had, and now live.

The promise

The parrot says, 'Good morning', from its pen,
The menu is open in front of us
And I am in the world of choice again,
A solace, and all its promises.
If I were a doctor I would harness more
The power of self-prescribing, it brings
A sense of autonomy, of growth, the core
Is stimulated again and my tired heart sings.
It gives my self a chance to recalibrate,
To sift through what I feel and what I know,
Let melancholy in and then what fate
May choose to find for me, to show.
I rattle like buttons in a toffee tin,
I need to sort them. So let me in.

3

Gansey Girl

(a modern sculpture in Bridlington Harbour)

I sit and wait. I gaze, I hope, I knit.
This is my place, you can find me here
In evening shadows or early morning fret
When mist curls and the sun begins to stir
I know the shape of boat and shape of man
As well as I know my own mirror face,
My searching eye finds them, it always can
And my pulse settles to a steady pace.
For this knitting can forge a future now
Waiting with an already broken heart
Ready to be mended each day somehow,
The talisman I create in woollen art.
So I sit and wait as we have always done
Needles clicking as if dice are thrown.

4

So the park

So the park, small, urban, bounded by train,
The sanctuary of trees and grass
From where mosque and church can be seen
Above the roofs of shop and house.
The paths through, the ceremonial gate,
The bandstand, bowling green, the tennis courts
All asleep still, only a dog walker might
Be seen, a squirrel full of squirrel thoughts.
And me. Large old man on bike sweeping past
In a fleece wearing hi-viz majesty,
Those caught glimpses are ones that last,
Recollected in tranquility,
The rooting of my soul in this beloved town
Ever strengthens, radical and deeper down.

5

Today, the cycle ride

Already yesterday's news the bike ride
Followed our usual route into town
Along the canal bank, we tried
To stay upright, not fall in or drown.
We wore our old blokeness with pride,
Crying out our fealty to the crown,
God for Charlie, England, St George. I lied,
Delete those last lines they are not true,
A weak attempt at satire which fell flat,
We pedaled to lunch as we always do
With the occasional half-shouted chat.
And as a poet I must be dutiful
In my reporting; it was beautiful.

The veg shop

Virtue is what I feel, the warrior of fruit
And cauliflower, the hero of the hour.
I've got you apples, each rosy new recruit,
Satsumas; I have you in my power,
Bananas are gathered and grapes; you're mine.
Comes the man and then comes the hour
Let battle commence, I give the victory sign
Be bold, be brave, do not cower.
I am a Quaker, war does not sit well with me,
I should flinch from use of martial terms
And violent battlefield imagery,
This is not a genuine call to arms
Just a celebration, a lighthearted plea
To witness my joy in Vitamin C.

Bottle bank

I love the glorious smashing of glass
At the bottle bank, a simple pleasure
Heightened by do-gooding, top of the class,
Peak experience of my semi-leisure.
Panniers full I cycle and clink
To my destination by the Co-op,
I want to tell folk that I don't drink
But it would seem hollow in this glassy drop
Of wine bottles, jam jars and other flasks,
The detritus of living, the left-over bits,
This is a favourite of my tasks,
Getting rid of stuff that gets on my tits.
And let me emphasise to allay any fears
I don't drink and haven't for years.

8

Car Boot

We sit with coffee and watch the crowds
Mill around the bustling car boot ground,
Me and the hound, rather taken by the hordes
Of customers for shite, circling round.
All drawn by the chance of a special find,
The Kohinoor amongst the paste and brass,
The antique which will blow the collective mind
Of every auctioneer, the lottery win, the next class,
And then the sun comes out and I see joy,
The collector of possibilities.
This is an ancient marketplace, where boy
And girl trade across the centuries.
What price would fetch my urban cynicism
When all around is happy (sorry!) jism.

9

Here I am

Here I am, just present at the table,
Not quite on duty yet, but still ready
To respond as far as I am able,
Anxious but somehow holding steady.
I've been invisible these last few weeks
Haunting my own life and barely even there,
The sense of weeks of troughs, no peaks,
Of an exposed soul, small, shivering bare.
But there is no huge self-renaissance,
No reborn, saccharine win, win, win
But a tiny and yet real recompense,
Paper-round money in the scheme of things,
And in all the fogged blur of recent days
I see myself clearly, quite free of haze.

We wander

And we wander amongst the grave stones
You a squirrel hound (in your doggy dreams)
Me looking for the stories and the bones
Of meaning to be found in churchly schemes,
To always remember the dead, hold them
Forever in marble and granite love,
Not allow for covering in moss and ivy stem
The muffling of their voice, leaves from above.
But here are signs of earthier pleasure
Against the church wall around the back:
The wine glass, condom, earring which measure
The life force of an urgent drunken fuck.
Doggie and I see the mundanity
Which in their moment seemed eternity.

Green

There is a force of colour whose rhythm a drum,
If a colour can be a sound it is a song,
It's dewy cool and damp against your skin
It is taste of new season, zest of spring
It is fresh mint that tingles on your tongue
The flicker of a light which teases your eyes
The sound of early birds waking to sing,
The melody of the new against the palest of skies.
A punch to the chest, like nothing else could.
It fills you like the best, nourishing meal
It generously paints you hills and wood,
And when it seems there's nothing more to feel
Its guitar strings strum lightly in your heart
Green leaves of music, in composer's art.

So many fears

My life is now made from many frights,
Small fears that swell and magnify
in the sharky shallows of the nights,
When it all becomes so tough to try,
When past courage seems too frail and thin
To do more than remind me what is lost
And through the water cuts a killer fin.
I fret at the hypothetical cost
But I try to do most things anyway,
Just do them, with gritted teeth and steely jaw.
There comes relief with each day
That I achieve what I need and much more.
Is it the frailty that comes with the years
Or was I once better at hiding my fears?

Robert Frost

Robert Frost, esteemed poet, Robert Frost
You're in my ears when I do humble tasks
In house or garden, I have my fingers crossed
In case somebody stops me and asks
Are you a fan of the aforesaid man
Who wrote about the daily, little stuff
And somehow constructed a master plan
To show how small, how huge, how enough
Our everyday life could be, how we decide
One way or another and how that affects
The path we choose to take, the road we ride
And every other little reflex.
I cut the grass today and I was lost
In your world again, blessed Robert Frost.

14

This place is ballast to my soul

The Leeds Library

This place is ballast to my soul, which rights
Itself in seconds of being here.
It promises peace and calm, it excites
The tiny muscles in my eyes and ear.
I sit at an old table and sip tea
Looking around at what I know so well,
Books in all their variegation I see,
The desk where I once studied, the spell
Still captures what lingers and remains
After this slow erosion of my very self.
I am a barely covered bag of old bones
Who limps while still looking from shelf to shelf.
Everything changes that we know
This place not so much somehow.

Such a small dog

Such a small dog, miniature hound
Whose nose was bred a sniffing snout,
How big do these new words sound:
'A rabies jab', before we take her out
Under the sea on the train to Normandy,
Lap-bound until we reach the other side,
Rejoin our car and drive off to see
The pleasures of Norman countryside.
We sit in the waiting room until our turn,
Will it be a large needle? I never stare,
Too late for stoicism, to learn
A new courage while with her there,
Such a small dog, miniature hound
You are rubber, you will rebound!

You have left

You took a long time to say goodbye
We relished each day as an extra gift
Six months going, we all knew why,
Weeks of laughter, we were adrift
In a sleepy lagoon and floating free
Gathering ourselves for the final end
It would happen inevitably.
The tissue would stretch and tear and rend
And now you are no longer here
The urge to ring you not gone away
Expecting a door knock, you to appear,
I think of you at least once every day.
Oh, the weight of you both light and heft
We said long goodbyes, I am not bereft.

A calendar of events

I have a calendar of events:
Having coffee with friends and catching up,
Occasional work and stuff prevents
The purposelessness, the empty cup.
For each time I struggle with a key
To get it in the door, lose a name
A little chilly stir can frighten me,
This might be a signal of my final game.
So these small arrangements, these little joys
Can hold off the plunder each year makes
Faster now than ever, no warning noise,
Each week races and then overtakes.
Living in the now, the minutes as they pass,
Though coffee can't deny, all flesh is grass.

Witness

Write it down, witness it, you will forget,
You think you won't but you always do,
Memory is short, mercifully, yet
Sometimes we should record the true,
The important, before time steals
The small, real signs of our humanity,
The warmth of the sun, how love feels,
Birdsong that begins and ends each day.
For I can still connect to another's words
From thirty or three hundred years ago
The brightness of their hope, the warning clouds,
What I feel now is and was always so.
Little stays in this shifting transience,
Human experience caught and made sense.

Lost

All was lost or so it seemed to this man
Tired of being brave, surviving grief
Trembling on the edge of old age, no plan
In deep despair from which was no relief
And then the messages started to come,
Unrelated, kind folks sending them,
Connecting, the beat of a faraway drum,
Chlorophyll rising in the stem.
Somehow I feel the confidence of hope,
Connection to another human heart.
It may not last, it may turn off and stop
It may just make a grand depart.
But in these old and more fragile states
It gives me hope, love resonates.

Shirt

This is my favourite summer shirt,
I'd wear it every day if elves came
And washed it in the night, freed it of dirt
Ironed it and hung it for me to claim.
Its paisley pattern pleases, makes me think
Of a summer of love fifty years ago,
I'm wearing it today while I sit and drink
In a cafe where Beatles songs ebb and flow.
I'll not overegg the significance
That certain clothes can bring with them, it's clear,
My change of mood is the evidence
The joy of patterns, oh how they cheer.
To be honest, I really must try more,
I picked it dirty from the bedroom floor.

Hair envy

The boy in the cafe has new hair
Cut in a way that expresses youth and style.
It's his third in as many weeks, not fair
If hair is something you've not had a while.
The boy in the cafe smiles at everyone
He serves, he seems uncomplicated,
Life for him is light and fun,
His movements deft and syncopated
But I remember those days so well,
It was not always lightness and joy,
Easier to present a glossy shell
While inside you're still just a boy.
So style it out, enjoy your new hair
While you may, while it is still there.

Oblique

Is best, don't look them in the eye,
Sometimes direct doesn't reach quite the same
As an inference, which fish hook can pry
And lock into lip and jaw and that's the game
Of poet or the one I try to be –
I hope to snag with words a heart and head,
To get as close, to feel your breath on me,
To know you feel mine, the artist's art.
But all ambition ends in another fail
Where the painter can't render what they see
And I am drifting without a sail
Exhausted by the necessity.
The need to try is baked into my soul
Like clay that's fired from the potter's wheel.

Blackbird in the Evening

This is for those with whom I fell in love
Mostly catastrophically, it's true,
Not many managed to break through and move
My teenage and young man's heart, then you
Came along by chance in the evening time,
Like a blackbird lighting up with sudden song,
A surprise visitation, a perfect rhyme,
The couplet I waited for all along.
And there are very few lessons to be learned
In a busy and eventful span,
Sometimes I've been frozen, sometimes burned,
Always hopeful though when I can.
This twilight gift cannot promise light
But holds at bay the coming of the night.

Missing

When I started to stop missing you
Ten years had passed and history rewrites
Itself and things assert and become true,
Are seen for what they, the wrongs and rights
Blur. But I still feel the amputation
And the loss, the damaged portions of my heart
For me my honourable reputation
Within myself, hoping that repairs will start.
After twenty years the pain has mostly faded
I feel the loss but hardly recognise
What it is, for I have finally traded
Those old feelings for new skies.
Thirty years and you have finally gone
Though still here, the echo of a song.

Ego

The instances of the use of 'I'
In the conversations of the young
Are many, I was as guilty in my
Boyhood as any other, it was sprung
From a place of forging identity,
Into who you might and could become
Where each usage made it easier to see
Who you are and, like a marching drum,
Took you into the world, the adult battlefield
And onto new things where discoveries
Could be made, and who you are, annealed
Like a sword hardened by self-victories.
I use 'I' less, don't need to identify
Or share quite so much how I signify.

Oak tree

So the sun comes and all the wild flowers
Along the roads and on the roundabouts.
For the year is hurrying, weeks like hours
And months like days. As time routs
Me, I'm standing, branches out, leaves bright
And ready but the passing of time blunts
My resolve, takes my strength, brings night
And I become the hunted lost to chance
For I was once a tall oak tree who stood
In a copse with the owl as my friend,
And I never thought that I ever would
Witness my triumphs and my flagging end.
I stand less tall and more crooked now
Waiting for the last chilly wind to blow.

Hallam

I stand here rooted in Christian earth
So many children lost, gone one by one,
Weighing up each loss, seeing their worth,
'Tis better to have loved' wrote Tennyson,
So I stare seeing past and future here
Crowded with the works of those gone before
Ears cocked to hear faint music in the air
Of other voices on each foreign shore.
I had purpose, a keen engaged eye,
The robes and books of learning hang on me,
I had an eagle's reach, soaring high,
Scanning below the maps of history.
Though hammer blows have cracked my heart
See me unshaken in my faith and art.

Rustling

The soundtrack of our long life together
Is full of the rustling noise you make
As you search for things that have no tether:
Debit cards, keys, notes (for fuck's sake)
And now you search the house for me
Under cushions, pillows and in the bed
Perhaps warm from where the dog used to be.
And then you search outside the house instead
Am I caught up high in the wintry trees
Like a flapping bin-bag waving down?
Am I on a bench, rug around my knees,
Waiting for a bus going into town?
This may be a fruitless, endless quest
Just rustling through stuff, hoping for the best.

St Michael's Churchyard

We nose amongst the gravestones, dog and I,
Inside, a choir sings a Christmas song
While I read the names of lives gone by,
Sometimes the past and present get along.
The old church music always comforts me,
I hum along to carols that I know
Amongst angels of stone and memory.
The dog just wags her silly tail. The flow
Of choir and life practice are much the same,
Follow the line, attempt to read the tune,
And if we stray, lose ourselves, try again;
Here my path is steady, I'm nearly done.
Trusting the faithful find what they might seek,
I feel the lightest feather brush my cheek.

Spring (they/them)

Spring comes mooching around the corner, late,
Does not apologise but does that trick with green
Where trees and hearts light up, inflate
With joy and I mark them in as seen.
For I keep the register, and they're here
With a coronation flummery,
The something special in the air,
The yearly budding, leafing ceremony.
My blood is slow to heat these days
And winters can feel so hard and long
But sitting here on my step, the vivid haze
Of growth, the blue sky, the black bird song.
All will be well, my aching bones will warm,
Forget the days of rain and winter storm.

Eradications

There have always been eradications
Of language, culture, race and history
For we humans like simplifications
To see just the things that we want to see.
How uncomfortable to realise
The history has been mostly shaped by men
A narrative they would not see as lies
Wanting things to be as they've always been
I reject all this, this erasion of women, of race
Of the queer, disabled, marginalised,
The gifts we have given, the sheer grace
Of our lives to be memorialised
This is what art must do, remember, reclaim
And who and what we are, give it a name.

Old Lad

Younger than me, perhaps the oldest paper boy,
A man of simple pleasures, a pint, his dog,
He has died. Is dead. Let's not be coy
Never quite well, his feet, his heart a bog
Of damaged tissues, but still so kind
A man of smiles and such good cheer.
When my paper arrives he comes to mind,
Sunshine in the rain, a smile beneath a tear.
So wherever you are now, old lad, be well,
Take pleasure in this quiet and peaceful while.
You will be in pub heaven, certainly not in hell
With a permanent bacon-sandwich smile.
No more deliveries on your poorly feet,
Take a long break, you've earned the right.

Hearts Heal

This is for the people who did not love us,
Did not know how, or could not show it
Or perhaps felt nothing, no low-key buzz
Of connection. Then went on to blow it.
The harm they did perhaps not caring,
The American term 'ice-box' seems apposite
In the room, door open, always whirring,
A cold draft chilling, a frosty blight.
But if you did care but could not see
How to let us know, I did survive,
Made my family from those around me,
Found another life of my own to live.
The word forgiveness is not needed or true
For hearts heal, and have little need of you.

34

Train

There's no recovery from this dis-ease
No snapping back to health like elastic
At no time is it just a spiffing wheeze,
I can't be recycled cardboard and plastic.
Instead I find myself marveling at the number,
The station at which my steam train will arrive,
I am dead old, the years encumber
And I will soon be seventy-five.
But, and there's always a 'but' in sonnetry,
I breathe, and hear and see. I touch, smell and taste
I live in fact, take part, my world is still me
I can afford to slow down, no need for haste.
One day there'll be no stopping of the train
I'll chug into the sunshine after the rain.

35

Men who shave too often

My father's definition of 'the gays'
In his army years, does not need to soften,
Unprejudicial even nowadays
Just men who perhaps 'shaved too often'.
As an avid shaver I can concur
But how would he describe those at my gym
Perfect of eyebrow, hair with no flaw,
What would such men mean to him.
I have no gaydar, do not really know
Whether they are gay or completely straight,
Statistics suggest they are hetero
Just careful of how they presentate.
So father, dear father perhaps times have changed
The dandies of today may not be gay.

Otto

I glimpse him in the alleyways, the park,
Sometimes wandering along the promenade,
It is the ghost of him, a shadow in the dark.
Who knew, four years on, missing would still be hard.
He's gone into eternal Pets at Home
Where all his canine wants and needs are met,
Always a cushion or a rawhide bone,
Pooch heaven where the sun will never set.
But thankyou Spanish city for the ghost
Of the ambling, standard sausage dog
We see everywhere, found not lost
The simple proof that there is a god.
Finally the Crufts of time has decreed
Of all the dogs he came out best in breed.

Prosopagnosia

I have it; not infectious, not passed on
Through touching. Something always part of me
The vagueness my life is founded upon
Just not recognising the face in front I see,
Put on a woolly hat and I have no chance
Beards or spectacles are just the same,
My mind goes into the whirling dance
Looking at the face, not finding the name.
Once at a book signing I asked how to spell
A name of someone I did not recognise
It didn't exactly end very well
A, double N, Ann not a surprise.
So if I look vague, as if my mind has gone,
You're lost from my facial lexicon.

Apparently

Apparently it's the eyes which go first,
The easiest to peck out, I'd say,
And that would probably be the worst
And I would be quite dead anyway.
This battlefield would be still, a hush
After clashing blades and painful cries
And I'd lie here, no more need to rush,
Carrion for crows and ripe fruit for flies.
And do not doubt if I were left out there
Foxes would come and go to town
Smaller scuttlers with teeth all sharp and bare
Except for bones the rest would compost down
But make no mistake you do not need to care
Whoever I was will not be there.

You gave me a box

You gave me a box (at seventy-five),
A Victorian caddy with a key.
To celebrate how long I'd been alive,
To keep secrets safe, or a memory.
But looking at it now I wonder what
Thought I might trap there, a pinned butterfly,
A pressed flower, forget-me-not
The colour of a fresh-washed sky.
But then this morning in the park
I saw an April tree, a green flame
Of fresh leaves glowing in near dark
While others still bare in winter shame.
I need no box to keep such memories
Just fourteen lines with words as keys.

Compost

I take the compost out every day,
The peelings, cores and tea bags too.
A certain smugness in the way
I parade to the bin, look at the good I do,
I'm saving the planet one leaf at a time
Or at least the good earth of Leeds 6.
The rats are in on my little scheme
Each journey provides them with snacks
But like everything these days I see
(In my old man's walk, in the mossy lawn)
Intimations of my own mortality,
Hear the distant sound of hunting horn
I will compost, I will return to earth,
It was predestined even from my birth.

London Train

The Leeds to London train, chugging through
The periods of my fifty plus years of adult life
The blur of towns through which I knew
The accreted memories of joy and grief.
My face in the window reflecting back
An older wiser, not quite gentleman.
The light on meadows in spring attack,
My body answers as best it can.
For these are the arteries and veins
Of a life lived the very best I could
And this journey pumps and drains
The circulation of my blood.
How many more such journeys will be done?
It matters not, just this that I am on.

Goodbye

Saying goodbye can be a fucked-up thing
Station platform, in the street, hospital bed,
I thought I'd pass by all that, be the king
Of farewells and say it now instead
To all who I've loved (and sometimes hated)
All who touched my life, or just resented,
To anyone I hurt or soothed, perhaps dated,
Accept a virtual hug, Hermés scented,
For I am wrapping up the sleeping bag,
Scrubbing out the beans from the billy-can.
Folding the tent, it had begun to sag,
Leaving behind the ancient man.
I look forward to the peace a bit further on
The glories of complete oblivion.

43

Horses

May you find horses to ride on the moor,
To breathe the heathered air, and feel them move
Beneath you, carrying you, while skylarks soar
And dip above. This union can prove
That you still live, help you find a way.
You cling on carried by a gentle beast,
The steaming air, the scent of leather and of hay
When morning is a blessing and a feast
For the past trots close behind, always there.
The present is what we have, must endure
The future dim in dark and starlight air,
Only the horses know and keep our actions pure.
May you find your own salvations to ride,
May they bring you comfort, and be your guide.

44

Yellow tooth

Wobbly for months, at the back of my mouth
Touched by my tongue, second by second,
Just fell out, unplugged and went south
Sooner than I had untimely reckoned.
Tombstone like, or an old mossy stone
Grinding my food for seventy-five years.
I feel dental guilt, think I should atone
Is this just a beginning (one of my fears)
But in the end my mouth feels peaceful,
It's happened, no sense of impending doom,
No sense that I am somehow disgraceful,
My tongue may wander, it has much more room.
Now it's in a dish by the side of the bed,
Like a dinosaur's bone, recently dead.

45

Letter to my father

Imperial War Museum, 1956

You took us there so many years ago
The boys on that long journey underground,
We passed bombsites with only buddleia to show,
Soon to be built over, lost and then found.
Inside a museum quiet and cool,
A muted hush of recent history,
My seven year old self nobody's fool
But not knowing what we were there to see.
It was only later, much later, days ago
I realised that the triumphal pomp
Was camouflage for something below
I heard echoes of the army camp.
You had taken us there so we could feel
What you had felt, to make it real.

46

There's an arrow falling through the air

Directionless and at the very end
Of its journey, and then resting there
All targets missed, can I just resend
It or should I let it lie half-buried
Like a pheasant feather on the grass,
Its tip sparkling and as yet unbloodied
While careless folk just talk and pass.
For those arrows were my future hope,
I bent the bow and somehow set them free
Each one with a prayer that I escape,
Each one carrying the heart of me.
Something, point or flight, it can't be denied
Finally let me down. At least I tried.

Creaking

I creak with age and responsibility
Mostly to my poor shattered self,
I need to treat myself more tenderly,
Make room for forgiveness, mental health.
There is no arrival, no 'made it' place,
No Nirvana, sense of eternal bliss,
Just the daily struggle, the deep mill race
I find myself in, I struggle to confess.
But in my quiet embarrassed talks with God,
As if to an uncle I hardly know,
I face my own faults, give them a nod,
Feel my heart expand, beat fast then slow,
I am old now, have not always been kind,
Must forgive myself, leave the shit behind.

48

Rhubarb

I am a poem, and my creation
A hidden secret born of the night,
Has a tender, ruby-crowned elation
Hatched in the dark and picked by candlelight.
I am an enigma, a mystery,
Was grown in flat fields by the river's side
In sight of the Abbey's millstone history,
Fruit, vegetable, it's hard to decide.
Rattling to London on the rhubarb train
From Leeds and Bramley and onto the Ritz.
I was not merely a Yorkshire refrain,
But one of the kitchen's greatest hits.
Though a poet's doorstep can be my end
An allotment present from their artist friend.

49

It may not be balance, just a flat tyre

I've been wobbling a few days on my bike,
Often when I slow and turn the handlebars,
It makes me wonder if perhaps a trike
Would make me safer in a world of cars.
My balance seems to be retreating,
I hate this feeling of being insecure,
Is this it, an inner voice is tweeting
Am I at the beginning, is there no cure.
But I argue with myself (not out loud)
And think that I must check my wheels.
It could be nothing, these thoughts that crowd,
But perhaps this is what everyone feels.
Actually my tyres just needed pumping,
Note to self, less conclusion jumping.

Quiche

If quiche was my last supper it would please
If it were mine own, pastry crisp and thin
Heavy cargo of cauliflower, cheese,
Butterbeans, onions would also be in,
With a side of new spuds and asparagus.
A feast truly fit for queens and kings
With the extra bang, the super plus:
Leftovers for what the next day brings.
But if that was not possible let it be
Take away fish, chips, ketchup, at North Beach
Parked up facing the chilly sea,
Flamborough cliffs, misty, just out of reach.
Our lives are made up of last things and times,
I fix mine in a sonnet's beat and rhymes.

Plaque

The Hyde Park Picture House

We find it in the delicious pre-film hush
As we bend to scan the backs of seats,
Phone torches on before any rush
To find 'my plaque' which now completes
Fifty-three years of coming and sitting here
In the old picture house above.
But this new room it is now clear
Cements my history with a place I love
For my name on a seat offers an extra span
Beyond whatever time I'd left for me,
The line of my poetry humbles this man
And has much more emotional heft for me.
I sit in the waiting dark to witness how
I'm here, and maybe for a little more now.

Nijinsky on a bike

I am not Nijinsky, not meant to be
But that moment of one leg in the air
To clear the saddle, that was me,
Almost didn't make it over there.
To be honest I wobbled like a reed
In the wind, thought that I might fall
But something balletic in my hour of need
Steadied me, allowed me safety after all.
But perhaps it's time to recognise
Such gymnastics could be the death of me
And it may be practical and wise
To ride a bike that is quite crossbar free,
And that I will not be dancing any time soon
In Debussy's *Après Midi d'un Faun*.

53

So we talked

for Elaine

We spun webs of our present and our past,
Me on my bike, in the street face to face,
And it was a celebration. We held fast
To good things. It was a holy time and place.
We talked of children, or what we held dear
Of schools and friendship, the human space.
These were the common threads that drew us near,
The history which seemed to hold us and bless.
To learn later that you were suddenly gone,
That inexplicably you were no longer here,
Was cruel, that your presence now was done,
Made our meeting sweet, sharp, somehow more dear.
But know this, for some or for many days,
You touched all our lives in different ways.

Billy

With a stone above him to try and stop
Any grave-robber fox just passing by
From snuffling and rooting to dig him up,
I hope his sleep is deep, and warm and dry.
The Converse box just about big enough
To contain his body, curled soft and tight,
After an ending which is quick and rough,
He's not marked, heart perhaps just burst with fright.
And much heavier in his death than life,
As I hold him bundled in my arm,
And somehow much more present in my grief,
While I remember his long life, its calm.
The stone sinks a little each passing day,
As he settles deeper, and ebbs away.

Three sonnets from Kefalonia

55

1: Byron in Metaxata

Statue of Byron in the village square,
Handsome, battered, and long venerated,
Looking out with a damaged, searching stare
Over what he loved and celebrated.
He spoke and still speaks for everyone,
And the debts to this place we all share,
The stories and myths told and handed down,
All the old philosophy founded here.
But the isles of Greece will always be
Where he found his truest and safest home,
The misty mountains set in the still sea,
The place where we pilgrims have always come
In search of the things we've lost or miss
In the faint footsteps of Odysseus.

11: Argos

This was the way he, wily, travel-stained,
Came limping to where fishing boats were tied,
Looking around for what had still remained,
Tired eyes where hope and joy had almost died.
In disguise through villages of his youth
Recognised by no one but going home
What would be left, just the bitter truth
That, after twenty years, not much the same.
But then the corner of his house was near
A joyful rustle from a bed of rags and straw –
Argos had waited through each long year,
He wagged his tail, whined a last welcome now.
Then the sweet sadness of his bursting heart
As his swallow soul could at last depart.

III: Message from Kefalonia

Greece has many messages still to tell;
The old man in the taverna who said
That laughter would help us live long and well
All the while laughing as he dipped his bread;
The spell of sand and beaches, Ithaca,
The mountains curved in trees and mist
The changing colours, ribboned roads, the sea,
The sense of who's walked here in the past;
The coin I wear around my neck shines bright,
Has him on it; he arrived home at last,
I touch it as one would an amulet
And it will remind me to hope and trust.
I realise in the church's candle glow
'Hold fast' the only words I need to know.

Autumn

My hands are bark and twigs
While warm flesh and muscle
Glove your fingers.
I feel the pulse,
The summer movement of blood through
The root of your thumb
See it beneath your skin.

We stand in an open doorway
While outside
Leaves like rusty terriers tumble
Under white-boned birches,
Quarrelling at their tips
And bushes are clotted with
Crimson berries and scarlet hips.

And through the pewter of an autumn sky
In a temporary torch-beam of sunshine
I see fruit like yellow light bulbs
Amongst the half-stripped silver leaves
Of an apple tree nearly over.

But you have to go.

Stay a moment more with me
Warming my hands in yours
Before, howling, I blow into winter.

Notes

3: 'Gansey Girl' – a modern sculpture in Bridlington Harbour by the massively talented artist Stephen Carvill. It depicts a girl looking out to sea while knitting a fisherman's sweater, known locally as a gansey. It contains a whole story, and many stories, in its beautiful incarnation.

8: 'The Kohinoor' – One of the largest cut diamonds in the world, looted from Delhi and given to Queen Victoria in 1849.

27: 'Hallam' – This poem was written as part of a commission based around the monuments in St. Paul's Cathedral; '50 Monuments in 50 Voices'. Henry Hallam was an eminent historian (1777-1859), the father of Tennyson's great friend Arthur (1811-1833) to whom he dedicated his poem 'In Memoriam'.

50: 'Rhubarb' – This poem was commissioned to celebrate the blue plaque unveiling for Joseph Whitwell, rhubarb farmer of Hollybush Farm in Bramley, part of the so-called rhubarb triangle, whose rhubarb travelled all the way to the Ritz in London.

53: 'Plaque' – The marvellous Hyde Park Picture House was closed for a long time for renovations. It was possible to sponsor a seat in the new basement screening room. My partner David 'bought' a seat for me and had (by complete chance) part of the introductory poem to this collection engraved on the plaque along with my name.

55: 'Byron' – The great English Romantic poet who spent many years in Greece and is revered as a hero there.

56: 'Argos' – Odysseus' dog, who waited patiently for his master's return from the Trojan Wars in Homer's epic poem *The Odyssey*.